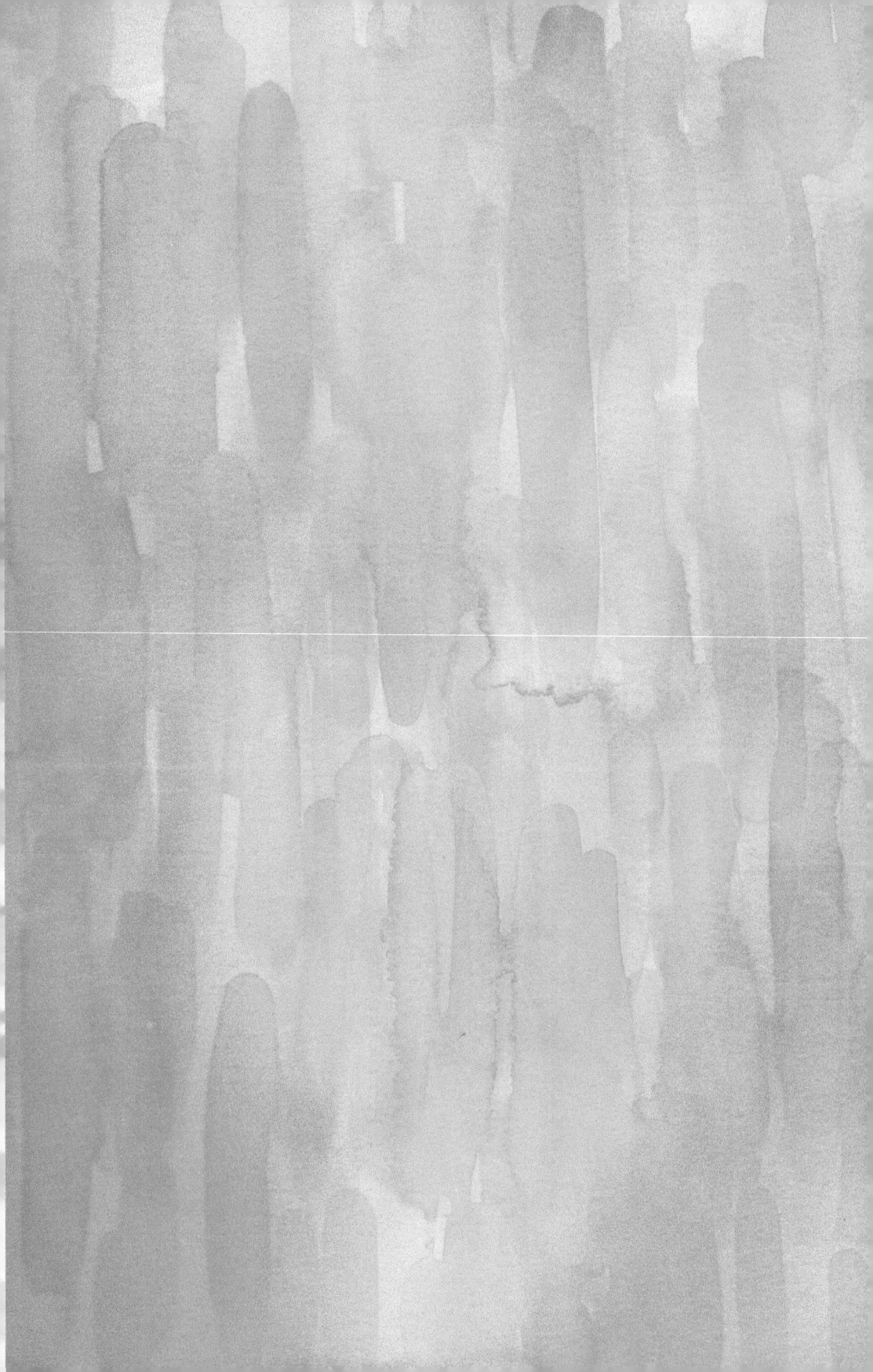

NO ONE POOPS EXCEPT YOU

written and illustrated by
Stephen Saff

Three Tries Press

No One Poops Except You

And Everybody Thinks It's Gross. Everyone.

by **Stephen Saff**

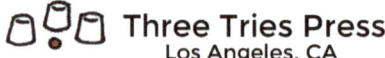 **Three Tries Press**
Los Angeles, CA

Library of Congress Control Number: 2024950048

ISBN Hardcover: 979-8-9916056-0-1

ISBN Paperback: 979-8-9916056-3-2

ISBN e-Book: 979-8-9916056-2-5

noonepoops.com

threetries.com

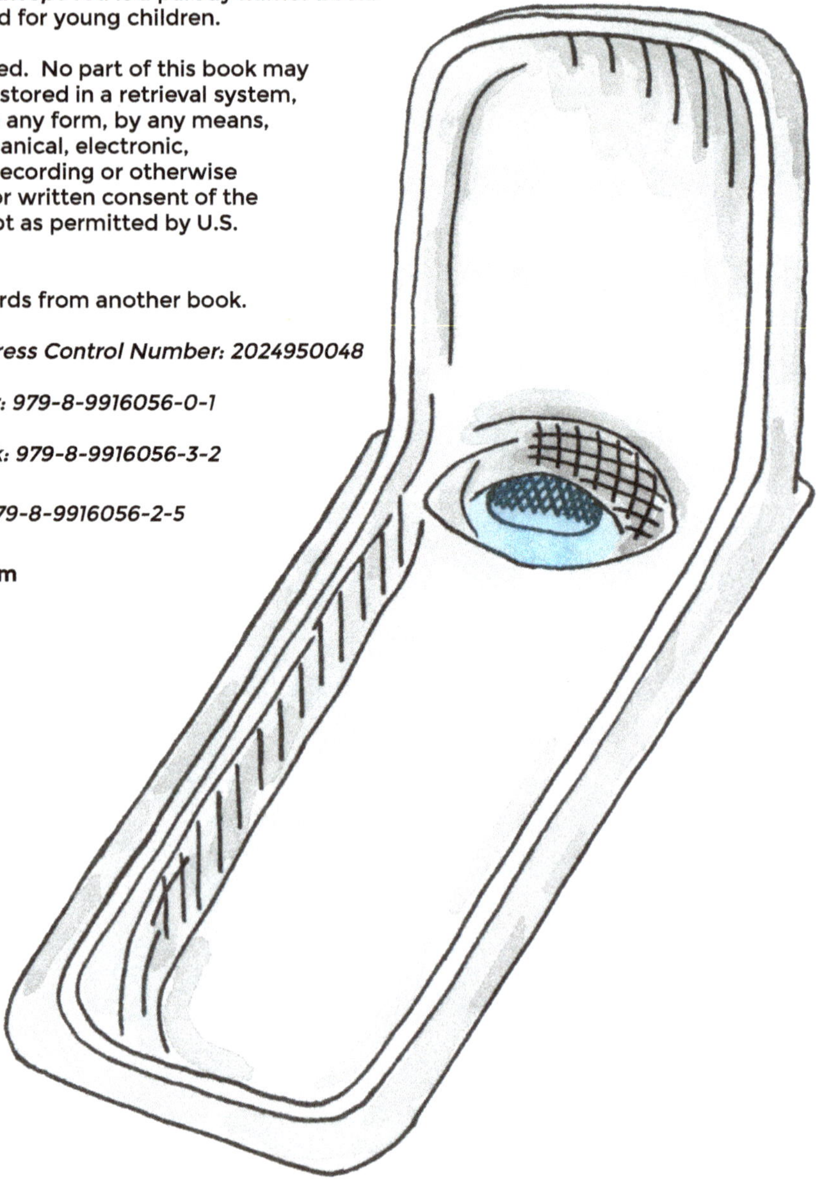

Dedicated to...

Just kidding
      You can't dedicate a poop book.

You are the only one who poops

When you poop

you poop alone

and it's gross

It's the grossest
thing in the
whole world

No one else in the world poops

Why are there so many toilets

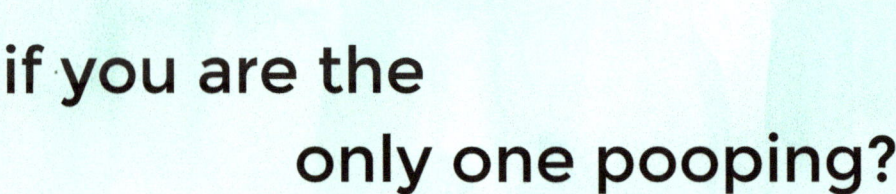

if you are the
only one pooping?

That's simple
They are all for you

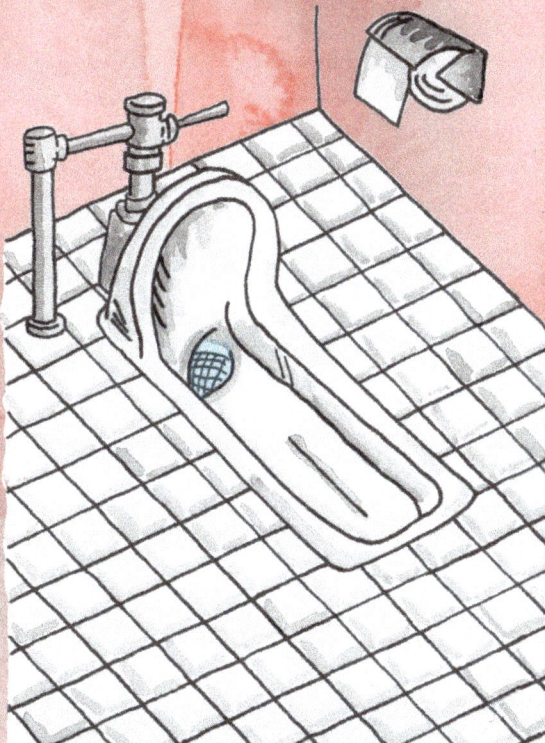

Sometimes you see other people's feet in the stalls

They are only
pretending
to poop

You are the
only one who
is actually
that disgusting

But you should
be crying because
you are alone

and stuff
comes out
your butt

Everyone else
eats food
and turns it
into energy

You just turn it into turds

While you are pooping all your family, friends,

and people
you have met
talk about
you and laugh

Even the animals know about your vile habit

"Ugh, I know
what that
smell means."

says the Hippo

They all laugh at you

You are a disgusting joke

And so is your poop

No one
poops
except
you

THE END

...Except for you
For you it never ends

www.ingramcontent.com/pod-product-compliance
Lightning Source LLC
Chambersburg PA
CBHW051650120626
46551CB00015B/2294